University Heritage Serie

The Ogam Stones
at University College Cork

Damian McManus

CORK UNIVERSITY PRESS

First published in 2004 by
Cork University Press
University College
Cork
Ireland

© Damian McManus and UCC Heritage Committee 2004

British Library Cataloguing in Publication Data
A CIP catalogue record for this book is available from
the British Library

ISBN 1 85918 320 4

Typeset by Tower Books, Ballincollig, Co. Cork
Printed by ColourBooks Ltd, Baldoyle, Co. Dublin

Contents

Acknowledgements

I would like to express my thanks to the Department of Early and Medieval Irish at University College Cork for their invitation to me to prepare this guide to the Ogam stones in the College. Very special thanks are due to Ms Virginia Teehan and Mr Michael Holland for their invaluable help in the preparation of the book.

The Rev. P. Canon Power's guide to the Ogams in the College (*The Ogham Stones; University College, Cork*, 1932) was of great assistance to me in my work. I am also indebted to Mrs Claire O'Kelly for a copy of her husband's *The Ogam and other inscribed stones at University College Cork* (M. J. O'Kelly, 1976), which was designed to bring Power's work up to date in Ogam studies and to facilitate the visitor to the College as structural improvements in the cloister had resulted in the relocation of some of the stones. Professor O'Kelly's work, unfortunately, was never published.

My greatest debt, as usual, is to my wife, Claudia, both for her assistance in reading the stones and for her patience with the work.

Damian McManus

Introduction

As our earliest written source of the Irish language, the oldest documentation of Irish personal names, indeed the earliest tangible evidence of Irish scholarship and learning, the Ogam inscriptions hold a place of considerable importance in the history of Irish letters. If their importance has been understated from time to time by some Irish scholars, who regarded them at worst as meaningless, or as forgeries, or dismissed the Ogam script as a mere cipher of the Latin alphabet, recent research has led to a more favourable appreciation of the achievement of the Ogamists, even if many aspects of their creation remain the subject of speculation. We will probably never know exactly when, where or why this peculiar script and its unique alphabet were devised, nor what inspired them, but we do know that from the Old Irish period (seventh–ninth century) until the demise of the native schools of Classical Modern Irish (seventeenth century) the Ogam system was the framework for the study of Irish letters and was regarded as uniquely Irish. According to one tradition inspired by the Biblical narrative on the creation of linguistic diversity (Genesis 11), and found in the early medieval Irish poets' primer, the *Auraicept na nÉces*, the Irish language (*Goídelc*) and its script (*Ogam* or the *Beithe-luis-nin*) were created from the best of every other language and designed specifically for the use of scholars. Propaganda, no doubt, with about as much basis in reality as the Genesis narrative itself, but the coupling of the language and Ogam as an inseparable pair is there together with the belief in the great antiquity of both. There too is the view that Ogam was designed as a vehicle for the Irish language, a thesis which has more going for it than some modern attempts to juggle it out of a Latin framework.

Orthodox Ogam (i.e. the Ogam of the oldest inscriptions, fifth–seventh centuries, as opposed to the so-called 'scholastic' Ogam of later manuscripts) used a series of twenty characters arranged in four groups, each group made up of one to five scores (often mere notches in the case of the last group) disposed to the

1

right or left or diagonally across a stemline (generally the edge of the stone, but an imaginary stemline in the case of rounded boulders), or cut on the stemline itself in the case of the notches. The system has much in common with the primitive tally and operates by marking position to a fixed series of sounds. Orthodox bilingual (Latin/Roman and Irish/Ogam) inscriptions in Wales, the Isle of Man, Devon and Cornwall provide the key for the majority but not all of those sounds and the later manuscript tradition fills in the gaps, though without confirmation from the early period this later evidence has to be treated with caution. In Fig. 1 the Ogam characters are presented in their traditional vertical format and are accompanied by the conventional values confirmed by the bilingual inscriptions. Fig. 2 shows the typical horizontal disposition of Ogam in the manuscript tradition together with the values accorded the symbols in that tradition.

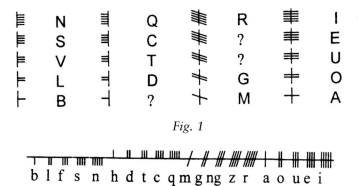

Fig. 1

Fig. 2

It will be evident that there is clear agreement between both traditions in the case of the majority of the Ogam characters, a testimony to the stability and continuity of the system from the earliest period. Changes such as that from Orthodox V to manuscript *f* reflect a development within the language between the Primitive (fifth–sixth centuries) and Old Irish (seventh–ninth centuries) periods and alert us to the fact that the manuscript record is a contemporary one and does not preserve the original values in cold storage. A safer guide to the latter will be found in the names of the letters themselves. These were meaningful words

2

in the language and can be shown to be of great antiquity. The idea that they were all names of trees is a late medieval fiction arising from the fact that the largest single semantic category among the letter names was an arboreal one, and the fact that by the later period a number of the letter names had become redundant except as names, their original meanings being lost or forgotten. Old Irish kennings on the names predate that fiction and are of the utmost importance for establishing their meaning, which in turn helps to establish their etymology, their form in the Primitive Irish period, and, by this somewhat circuitous route, the original value of the symbols reflected in the initial sound of the name. Thus, the name of the third symbol was *fern* 'alder tree' in Old Irish, and its kennings (*airenach fían* 'vanguard of warrior bands', *comét lachta* 'milk container' and *dín cridi* 'protection of the heart') point to the use of the timber of the alder tree as the material of shields and liquid vessels. The Old Irish form of the name in turn explains the manuscript value *f*. The word *fern* is cognate with Welsh *gwern(en)* 'alder tree(s)' and would have had the form *verna̅* in Primitive Irish, whence the orthodox value V. This method of investigation helps in our understanding of a number of unusual features in the manuscript tradition but some problems remain, either because the meaning of some names is still unclear or because etymologies have not been found for others.

The names of the letters are as follows:
Beithe 'birch tree', *Luis* 'flame/herb (?)', *Fern* 'alder tree', *Sail* 'willow tree', *Nin* 'fork'; (*h*)*Úath* 'fear', *Dair* 'oak tree', *Tinne* 'rod of metal', *Coll* 'hazel tree', *Cert* 'bush' *Muin* 'neck', *Gort* 'field', (n)*Gétal* 'act of slaying', *Straif* 'sulphur', *Ruis* 'red'; *Ailm* 'pine tree (?)', *Onn* 'ash tree', *Úr* 'earth', *Edad* (?), *Idad* (?).

As an alphabetic writing system Ogam, of course, cannot have been created in a vacuum but the overhaul of the alphabetic system which inspired its creators is complete, making the identification of the model frustratingly difficult. It is clear, however, that the Ogamists had some training in the properties of sounds; witness the separation of vowels from consonants and the coupling of related sounds (*d* and *t*, *c* and *q*) in the system. The absence of a symbol for the sound /p/ in the Ogam alphabet points in a similar direction. At the time of the creation of the system this sound was not current in the Irish language and there is surely no clearer indication that

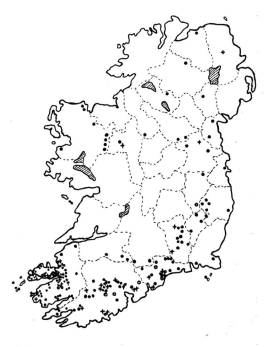

Distribution of Ogam inscriptions in Ireland.
● Single stone.
+ Group of 2–4 stones.
○ Group of 5 or more stones.

Fig. 3

Ogam was designed as a vehicle for the Irish language of its time than the absence of /p/ from the system. As the letter names date from the early period the sound /p/, though it is common later in loanwords and developed naturally in some native words through the devoicing of /b/, has had to make do in Irish with surrogate or artificially adapted names like *Beithe bog* 'soft b' and *Peithe*.

The distribution of the Ogam inscriptions (see fig. 3) has a marked southerly bias within Ireland. The counties of Kerry, Cork and Waterford boast approximately 260 stones out of a total in Ireland of about 330, more than one third of the overall total being in Kerry. There are very few stones with the Ogam character north of a line from Galway to Dublin. Outside of Ireland Ogam inscriptions have been found in Devon and Cornwall (7), Wales (40) and the Isle of Man (5). In the case of all of the above the language of the inscriptions in the Ogam character is invariably Irish, while

4

many of the Ogams in Britain are accompanied by contemporary equivalents in Latin, and in the Roman character, i.e. they are bilingual/biliteral. A number of inscriptions in Scotland also use the Ogam script but differ from those above in using a language other than Irish, viz. Pictish, or, according to the most recent study (Cox, 1999), Old Norse.

The distribution outside Ireland reflects that of the Irish diaspora of the fifth and succeeding centuries and some indication as to the fortunes of the Irish language among these settlers may possibly be gleaned from the gradual decline in the use of the Ogam script on commemorative inscriptions of this kind. The convention of using Ogam alone, which these settlers brought with them from Ireland, gradually gave way to the bilingual/biliteral type and finally the Ogam was abandoned, leaving only the Irish character of the personal names as a feature distinguishing these inscriptions from the native local ones.

Standard practice was to cut the inscription along the left-hand arris (edge) of the stone from bottom to top; long inscriptions go around the top and down the right-hand angle in boustrophedon fashion. Variations on this such as up-up readings or a disposition on the face of the stone are found, but are relatively uncommon. In Britain the standard practice is often abandoned in order to align the corresponding names in each script. The depth to which the scores are cut varies considerably; some will accommodate an index finger while others are hair-like scratches only visible under favourable light, and barely detectable to the touch of the finger.

The condition of the inscriptions today varies from stone to stone. Some are perfectly legible, others barely so, and many have some defect or other often caused by a secondary appropriation of the stone. For many of the Ogam stones have had a second life, mainly as building material in medieval (souterrains, ringforts, oratories, churches) and modern (outhouses, cottages etc.) constructions and have suffered in the adaptation to that purpose, though once trimmed for this new task they were at least from then on relatively safe from the effects of weathering, not to mention the intimacy of itchy cattle. In cases where the stone has had such a second life, of course, the original site of erection is not known, and some stones have been found in the most unlikely of places (e.g. in the bed of a stream, on a strand below the tide mark, buried in a

5

bog). Many were discovered marking modern graves in cemeteries or lying prostrate in fields and ditches. Some are associated with early structures such as stone circles, old burial mounds and cairns, while a small number of stones of megalithic proportions probably stand today where they stood when the Ogam was engraved.

With the possible exception of one stone in Wales, the people recorded on these inscriptions are not known from the historical record, with the result that absolute dating of the stones is impossible. Relative linguistic dating and a comparison with the forms of the Latin loanwords in Irish suggests that they belong to the period from Late Primitive Irish (fourth–fifth centuries) to Early Old Irish (seventh century). No inscription bears a form which would force us to push the dating further back in time than the fourth century, and no diagnostic Old Irish (eighth–ninth century) form occurs on them. The cult appears, therefore, to belong to the Christian period and to have gone out of fashion at the dawn of Old Irish, for whatever reason.

Some scholars (most notably the doyen of Ogam studies in the first half of the present century, R. A. S. Macalister) have held that the Ogam cult was a pagan one, the demise of which was a result of the triumph of Christianity, the triumph to which expression is given in the Prologue to the *Félire Óenguso*, where the glory of monastic settlements is contrasted with the ruin and decay of ancient (pagan) sites such as Tara and Emain Macha. Macalister's arguments in favour of the pagan character of the inscriptions were not very convincing and were based to a considerable extent on an imperfect understanding of their language, which he believed to have been archaic even at the time of writing, the preserve of a conservative druidic class which itself had invented the system. Crosses on the stones were dismissed as later additions designed to cleanse them of their paganism, while damage to other stones at the point where the name of the eponymous tribal ancestor should appear was interpreted as an act of what can only be described as Christian vandalism, the name being removed on account of its pagan associations. The language of the inscriptions, however, reflects developments which were taking place in the period of the cult and can hardly be described as an archaic register, while the crosses can occasionally be shown to be earlier than the inscriptions themselves. More to the point, one inscription records the station in life of its commemorand with the word QRIMITIR (gen. sg. of *qrimiter, Old Irish *cruimther* 'priest', from a Vulgar Latin form of Latin *presbyter*), which hardly lends support to the pagan school.

The convention in the Ogam inscriptions is to record the name of the person being commemorated (invariably a male in Ireland, once a female in Wales) in one of a set of formulae. The name of the person in question, though it generally comes first, is always in the genitive case, as are all names and formula words following it. The formulae are of the type X MAQQI Y '(stone/inscription/in memory of) X son of Y', X MAQQI Y MUCOI Z '(stone. . . of) X son of Y, member of the tribe of Z', X (MAQQI Y) AVI Z '(stone . . . of) X (son of Y) descendant of Z' etc. Occasionally one just finds a single name X '(stone . . . of) X'. Examples are:

GRILAGNI MAQI SCILAGNI '(stone . . . of) Grilagnas (OI *Grellán*) son of Scilagnas (OI *Scellán*).'

CATTUVVIRR MAQI RITTAVECAS MUCOI ALLATO '(stone . . . of) Catuviras (OI *Caither*) son of Ritavix (OI gen. *Rethach*) of the tribe of Allatis (OI *Allaid*).'

MAQI-DECCEDDAS AVI TURANIAS '(stone . . . of) Maqas-Decēdas (OI *Mac-Deichet*), descendant of Turaniā (OI *Tornae*).'

GOSSUCTTIAS '(stone . . . of) Gōsuctā (OI *Gúasacht*).'

Examples of bilingual inscriptions are (Latin first):

AMMECATI FILIUS ROCATI / [AM]B[I]CATOS M[A]QI ROC[A]TOS '(stone . . . of) Ambicatus (OI *Imchad*) son of Rocatus (OI *Rochad*).'

AVITORIA FILIA CVNIGNI / AVITORIGES INIGENA CUNIGNI 'Avitoria/Avi⁻torigia⁻, daughter of Cunignos (Welsh Cynin = OI Conán (< *Cunagnas*).' A nominative construction in Latin, mixed (gen. + nom.) in Irish.

It will be evident from the examples above that the language of the Ogams brings us back a considerable distance in linguistic history. The gen. (sg., of course, as we are dealing with personal names) case endings –I (o-stem), and –AS (consonantal stem) of forms such as GRILAGNI, and RITTAVECAS, for example, have disappeared (though not without trace) in the corresponding Old Irish forms *Grelláin* and *Rethach*. The form CATTUVVIRR preserves the compound nature of the name (*catus* 'battle' + *wiras* 'man') more clearly than its Old Irish descendant *Caither*, in which the composition vowel *u* has been syncopated and the initial *w* (Ogam V) of the second element lost by lenition. The form MAQI-DECCEDDAS = OI (nom.) *Mac-Deichet* shows the use of a different orthographical convention in Ogam (postvocalic D(D) = /d/, written *t* in Old Irish), while INIGENA preserves both the second and fourth syllables lost in Old Irish *ingen* 'daughter', though the lenited *g* in *ingen* (Classical Irish *inghean*), and the fact that the form itself (nom. sg.) is followed by lenition would confirm the former presence of these syllables for us. Finally the word MAQQI, Old Irish *maicc*, preserves the distinctive labio-velar sound /k^w/ now merged with /k/ and written *cc* in Old Irish.

It has already been pointed out that our manuscript tradition preserves an account, inspired by Biblical narrative, of the invention of both the Ogam system of writing and the Irish language. A separate tradition ascribing the invention of Ogam to Ogma mac Elathan of the Túatha Dé Danann is also attested, and here too the exclusivity of the system is highlighted in that Ogma is said to have created it as proof of his intellectual ability and with the intention that it should be the preserve of the learned, to the exclusion of rustics and fools. It is difficult to avoid concluding that this Ogma and Lucian's Ogmios, the Gaulish Hercules, are related, though there are some linguistic difficulties in the equation and the mechanics of the relationship between *Ogma* and *Ogam* are not clear. Early Irish saga also furnishes us with numerous references to the use of Ogam, though it is not clear whether Ogam here means anything other than 'writing', the use of the term being an accommodation to the time-scale of the sagas themselves. One standard type of reference makes a connection with the orthodox commemorative inscriptions as we know them. A formula of the type *cladar a fert íarom, sátir a lia, scríbthair a ainm n-ogaim, agair a gubae* 'his grave is dug, his headstone is fixed [in the ground], his name is recorded in Ogam and his keening is performed' frequently follows an account of the death of a hero in this material. More specifically, Early Irish legal texts refer to Ogam inscriptions (called variously *ogam i n-ailchib* 'Ogam in stones' or *int ogam isin gollán* 'the Ogam in the pillar stone') and give them official recognition as documents confirming title to land on the grounds, presumably, that the pillar-stone defined the boundary of the ancestor's territory as well as marking his grave.

The seventh century saw the end of the old orthodox use of Ogam as a monument script and from the Old Irish period on the scene shifts to scholarly activity in the domain of grammar and metrics. The paraphernalia of Ogam, the script itself, the order of the letters and in particular the letter names, were now a subject of study for trainee poets and grammarians. Conventional script had long since been adopted in this environment and these scribes and scholars showed admirable restraint in the use of Ogam in their manuscripts. A scribe might sign his name in the old script, another uses it to excuse mistakes arising from his hangover, but text in Ogam is always kept to a minimum. The 'Ogam tract' (In *Lebor Ogaim*) found, for example, in the *Book of Ballymote*, is something of an exception to this in its fascination with multiple versions of the alphabet, dismissed by Zimmer as 'wertlose Spielerei' ('useless dawdle'). Dawdle or not, this tradition kept a working knowledge of the script alive and paved the way for a revival of the monument tradition and a renewed interest in Ogam in more recent times. The Cork antiquarian John Windele records (in RIA MS 12 K 29, p. 314) an amusing example of a latter-day use of the script in county Cork, with which it will be fitting to finish this brief account of Ogam. A man named Collins from Duneen, Kinsale, had engraved his name on his cart in the Ogam character 'but the Police, not deeming this a compliance with the law, had him up before the Magistrates at Petty Sessions. On the evidence, however, of the Rev. Dan O'Sullivan, now P.P. of Iniskea, a most competent witness on all subjects pertaining to Irish literature, Collins was discharged but recommended by the magistrates to append on his cart shaft a translation for the benefit of County Gentlemen.'

The Ogams at University College Cork

The stones (27 in all)* in the cloister (or 'Stone Corridor' as it is familiarly known) on the North and West wings of the quadrangle in the National University of Ireland, Cork, constitute the largest collection of Ogam inscriptions on open display in the country. With the singular exception of stone no. 12, which is from County Waterford, all are from County Cork itself and were acquired by the College for the most part in the early decades of the last century.

The earliest acquisition by the College was of six stones which had been collected by the South Munster School of Antiquaries, in particular by the antiquarians John Windele (solicitor) and Richard Brash (architect), and were housed originally in the Royal Cork Institution (1807–61), a civic centre of public education modelled on the Royal Institution in London. On the dissolution of the RCI the stones were transferred to the newly established Queen's College Cork (1845). Five of these stones (nos. 1, and 20–23) are still on view; the sixth (P. 24, M. 135), from Knockourane (Mount Music, barony of West Muskerry) was in the College collection when Rev. P. Canon Power was writing (1932), but is now missing.

A further six stones (nos. 2, 3, 5, 6, 26a/b and 27) were discovered in 1911 acting as lintels (and in one case, no. 5, as a supporting stone) in a souterrain in the townland of Knockshanawee (parish of Aglish, barony of East Muskerry, mid. Cork). The souterrain was dismantled two years later by Prof. R. A. S. Macalister and Sir Bertram Windle, president of the College (1904–1919) and its first professor of archaeology (1910–1915), and the stones were transferred to the College. These inscriptions are characterised in particular by the faint scratch-like nature of their scores, a feature also of some of those from Ballyknock (see below).

Twelve (nos. 7–11 and 13–19) are from the townland of Ballyknock (parish of Ballynoe in the barony of Kinnatalloon, East Cork) where fifteen such stones in all were found acting as lintels in

---

*An additional stone, though lying in the Stone Corridor, is not on view and consequently is not discussed here.

a souterrain at Castle Farm. They were investigated by the Rev. E. Barry in the 1880s and were examined by R. A. S. Macalister in 1907. Thirteen of the fifteen were presented to the College in 1920 by the Duke of Devonshire, but one of these, the largest, was not transferred from Ballyknock.

Of the remaining four stones (nos. 4, 12, 24, 25) nos. 12 and 24 were found by Rev. P Canon Power (professor of Archaeology 1915–32) and were brought to the College by him for protection. No. 4 was probably acquired by Sir Bertram Windle in or around 1907, when Macalister examined it. No. 25 is not included in Power's account (1932) but was in the College in 1945, when Macalister published his *Corpus*.

The removal of Ogam stones from their original site of discovery and their transfer to the College has not been without its detractors. In particular, the acquisition of the Knockshanawee series by the College gave rise to bitter recriminations in a debate carried out in the pages of the *Cork Examiner* (*CE*) and the *Cork Free Press* (*CFP*) in 1913–1914. Sir Bertram Windle and Professor Macalister were accused by Dr Philip Lee (*CE*, Oct. 21st, 1913), who had described the souterrain in detail in the *Cork Historical and Archaeological Journal* (1911, p. 59), of an 'unpardonable outrage' in ruining the old souterrain and removing the stones from the site. Macalister (*CE*, Nov. 18th) defended the action on the grounds that there were any number of souterrains of this kind in the country, many of a far superior quality of construction and design to that at Knockshanawee, and in particular because the stones were removed for security reasons and in the pursuit of science, not to serve as road metal or roofing stone. He and Eoin MacNeill (*CE*, Nov. 19th) defended Sir Bertram Windle's efforts to establish at the College a collection of such antiquities where everyone interested in the national language could study its earliest available forms with the minimum of trouble. Indeed MacNeill considered it the 'duty of the nation' to collect these stones and house them in a museum, and he suggested that the Colleges of the newly established (1908) National University of Ireland would be an ideal home for such monuments, giving students of the language immediate access to objects of historical, philological and archaeological study. Some contributions (*CE*, Nov. 21st, 22nd, 24th, 25th) to Dr Lee's side of the debate were rather heated, accusing Windle of an 'atrocious act of vandalism' and imputing arrogance and elitism to the 'chosen University people', but the case for keeping such monuments *in situ* was probably best made by a Fellow of the Royal Society of Antiquaries of Ireland in an article which appeared in the *Irish Builder and Engineer* and was reprinted in *CFP* (Jan. 21st, 1914).

The convenience which a collection like that at the College affords the modern scholar and the casual observer does of course come at a price, and archaeologists today would probably be in favour of retention *in situ* wherever possible, once the scientific investigation of the stone had been made, and a cast taken. But anyone who has investigated Ogam inscriptions, and in particular faintly executed inscriptions like those from Knockshanawee, will know the importance of having a clear, unhindered view of all angles of the stone and will appreciate the desire on the part of the epigraphist to have as many informed opinions on them as possible. It is in this light that the reluctance on the part of Macalister and Windle to replace the stones where they found them should be viewed. They may have been guilty of excessive enthusiasm for the Ogams at the expense of the broader archaeological picture, but to accuse them of an act of vandalism sounds a little like axe-grinding, and was both ungracious and unfair. Many Ogam stones stand today in the most remote and isolated of sites, exposed to the perilous effects of weathering and far from the view of the interested observer. Here in Cork one can view a very representative sample of these monuments at one's leisure, happy in the knowledge that they are cared for and treasured by the College community.

The Ogam stones at the College are illustrative of a wide range of features associated with these monuments. Among these are:

(a) Variety in site of discovery. They were found, for example, as lintels or supports in medieval souterrains (the Ballyknock and Knockshanawee stones), as a lintel in a modern pig-stye (no. 22), built into an old church (no. 23), functioning as a gate-pier (24), in a bog (25) or on top of a cairn (12). Damage caused by secondary appropriation for building purposes is clear in the case of some (e.g. nos. 6 and 23).

(b) Variety in execution of the inscription, from faint or very finely scratched hair-like scores (the Knockshanwee stones, also nos. 11, 13 16) to deep scores such as nos. 4 and 18, deep and unusually long scores (no. 17), scores touched up (no. 22) and both faint and deep scoring representing two independent inscriptions on the one stone (no. 21). Similarly, one finds standard boustrophedon (i.e. up, top, down) readings on some of the stones, where the inscription is long enough to use both sides (e.g. nos. 4, 12), but no. 18 reads up both sides. Note that some stones are upside-down as they stand today (nos. 5, 22, 26a) and the inscription is on the rear angle in the case of others (no. 15, and the first inscription on no. 21).

(c) Variety in the types of name recorded and in the formulae. The three types of name commonly found on the Ogam inscriptions (A compounded dithematic, B uncompounded monothematic with or without suffix and C uncompounded dithematic of the structure MAQQI-X, where MAQQI does not express a filial relationship (i.e. 'son of X') but rather has the sense 'devotee of' or the like (e.g. Old Irish *Macc-Daro* 'devotee of the oak tree') are all here. Examples of A are: ERCAIDANA (no. 8), MEDDOGENI (no. 13), DOVALESCI (no. 21), CUNAGUS-SOS (no. 22); B suffixless: COLLI (no. 3), BRANI (no. 6), BROCC (no. 14), BAIT (no. 15); B with suffix: CARRTTACC (no. 1), BIRAC (no. 7) LUGUNI (no. 5), GRILAGNI, SCILAGNI (no. 9), BRANAN (no. 19), COLOMAGNI (no. 21); C: MAQI-ERCIAS (? no. 12), MAQI-TRENI (no. 18).

As for formulae, one finds (a) single name inscriptions (e.g. nos. 3, 8), (b) X MAQQI Y (e.g. nos. 5, 9, 16, 19), (c) the MUCOI type (e.g. nos. 4, 6), (d) ANM X (e.g. no. 13), (e) a possible AVI type (no. 21) and (f) a possible X Y patronymical genitive type (no. 12).

(d) Variety in the size of stone. Compare no. 2 with no. 14.

(e) The as yet not satisfactorily explained doubling of consonantal symbols (no. 1).

(f) A family relationship between persons recorded on stones from the same site, e.g. stones nos. 5 and 27, both from the souterrain in Knockshanawee, the person commemorated in each case being a son of (gen.) LUGUNI (nom. *Lugunias = Old Irish Luigne).

(g) The same element in the name of father and son (no. 12, ERC in this instance).

(h) Old and late inscriptions: the morphology of a number of

13

inscriptions is old, all case-endings being intact (e.g. no. 9, GRILAGNI MAQI SCILAGNI) while that of some is strikingly young, all case endings being lost (e.g. no. 16, CRONUN MAC BAIT).

A Tour of the Stones

We begin our tour of the stones with the first on the left as one enters the cloister through the main entrance on the North wing. Lower case letters in the transcription indicate hesitation or a degree of uncertainty with the reading, while square brackets indicate portions of the inscription no longer legible; letters enclosed in the latter represent the expected originals. Incomplete inscriptions are indicated by an ellipsis (. . .). The references at the end of each discussion are to the corresponding inscription numbers in R. A. S. Macalister's *Corpus Inscriptionum Insularum Celticarum*, vol. 1 (M.) and Rev. P. Canon Power's *The Ogham Stones, University College Cork* (P.).

1.   This stone served as a lintel in a souterrain in Barrachaurin in the barony of East Muskerry, Co. Cork. The structure was dismantled in 1845 and the stone, purchased by John Windele for £1, was first taken to the Royal Cork Institution and was later acquired by the College. The inscription is in fairly good condition, though incomplete, and reads up the left-hand side as follows: C[A]RRTTACC MMAQI Mo/u CAGg. . . In view of the doubling of consonants in the first name, known to the historical record as (nom.) *Carthach* (anglicised in (*Mc*)*Carthy*), the reading MMAQI seems preferable to Macalister's GAQI, which with the following MU, he explained as a 'deliberate camouflage of the tabooed formula MAQQI MUCOI'. This formula was followed by the name of the eponymous ancestor of the tribe to which the person commemorated belonged and Macalister believed it was viewed with disfavour by Christians. Whether this was the case or not, however, is questionable. The element CAGI appears elsewhere in the Ogam record but has not been identified in the manuscript tradition. If we have the same name here the Mo/u might be a reduced form of the possessive pronoun 'my', which appears in a special category of early Irish personal names. Ref.: M. 103, P. 26.

14

2.   This is the first of six stones from the souterrain in Knock-shanawee, barony of East Muskerry, Co. Cork; it served as the third lintel in the construction. The scores of the inscription, like many in the Cork collection, are faint (though not as faint as some others we shall see), making the reading difficult. R and G are sloped the wrong way, while M is cut at a right angle to the stem-line. The inscription, beginning just above the steel bracket, reads up the right edge of the stone as it now stands as follows: CULRIGAI MAQI MENUMAQ. . . The names here do not appear elsewhere in the Ogam corpus and identification is not certain. The -AI ending in the first is relatively uncommon; it appears again in the Cork collection (see stone no. 7). Ref. M. 115 P. 27.

3.   This is the second of the Knockshanawee stones and was the eighth lintel in the construction. The inscription is on the top right-hand side as the stone stands and reads up as follows: COLLI (though Macalister read OS for the final I). The word *coll* 'hazel-tree' is attested later as a personal name and is, of course, the name of the letter C in the Ogam alphabet. Ref. M. 117, P. 28.

4.   From a souterrain in Garranes, barony of Kinalmeaky, Co. Cork. The inscription is deeply cut and runs up the left-hand arris, around the top and down the right-hand side, reading as follows: C[A]SSITT[A/O]S maQi Mu[CO]I CALLITI. The CO of the third word is not clear but can be restored with reasonable certainty. The first name, whether with –AS (a consonantal stem) or –OS (an *i*- or *u*-stem) is not known from the later record; the second may correspond to the first element in the tribal name Cailtrige. Ref. M. 81, P. 25.

5.   This stone stood upright in the Knockshanawee souterrain supporting one of the lintels. As it stands today it is upside-down so that the text reads down rather than up. The inscription is light and neat and reads VEQIKAMI MAQi LUgUNI. Only four notches of the I of MAQI are clearly visible but the reading I is doubtless the intended one. The left-hand side of the scores of the g in LUgUNI are not visible. The K of the first name is represented by the first of the so-called *forfeda*, or supplementary characters, a series of five characters added to the original twenty. This is the only character of this series which is attested on the orthodox

inscriptions. The name LUGUNI is the most likely reading of the father's name on stone no. 27, which was adjacent to no. 5 in the Knockshanawee souterrain, so it is not inconceivable that the persons recorded on these two stones were brothers. The first name is not known from the later record; the second contains the element *Lugu-* (whence Old Irish *Lug*) and is attested, viz. *Luigne*. Ref. M. 113, P. 15.

6. This was the seventh lintel in the Knockshanawee souterrain. The inscription reads up the left-hand arris and across the top of the stone, where it breaks off. The reading is: BRANI MAQQi Mu[ ]C. . . Traces of scores are visible lower down on the right-hand arris, where Macalister read R[A]L. The third word was presumably the familiar formula word MUCOI and would have been followed by the name of the eponymous ancestor of the tribe to which the person commemorated belonged. This name, unfortunately, is now lost. BRANI corresponds to Old Irish *bran* 'raven', also attested as a personal name, and is the first element in the name BRANAN on stone no. 19 in the Cork collection. Ref. M. 116, P. 14.

7. This is the first of the series of stones from Ballyknock (see above). The inscription runs up the left-hand arris and across the top and reads BOgaI MAQI BIrAC. . . The G and A of the first word are difficult to read and the R of the last is damaged. The first name may stand in a similar relationship to the later attested *Bocán* as BRANI of stone 6 does to the BRANAN of stone 19; for the ending see the remarks on CULRIGAI, stone 2. The second name is probably the same as later *Berach*, an adjectival derivative of *bir* 'spear'. Ref. M. 89, P 5.

8. This is the second of the Ballyknock series and bears a single name on the left-hand arris reading up, ERCAIDANA. The elements in this compound name (*erc-* 'speckled' and *aidon-* 'fire') are well known from the Ogam record and from later sources, but this is the only example of their occurrence together, and this particular name is not attested later. Ref. M. 93, P. 4.

9. The inscription on this, the third stone from Ballyknock, is very finely scratched and the first two letters are difficult to make

out (most of their scores not being visible on the face of the stone), as are the finals of the second and last words. It reads up the left-hand arris as follows: grILAGNI MAQi SCILAGNi. Both names are of the structure stem + diminutive (formerly patronymical) suffix -gn- and both occur in later sources, as (nom.) *Grellán* and *Scellán*. In later Ogam inscriptions –AGNI may appear as –AN, as in stone no. 19 in the Cork collection (BRANAN from an earlier *BRANAGNI). Ref. M. 85 = P. 3.

10.   This stone from Ballyknock bears a short inscription on the right-hand arris reading up, C[O]VALUTi. The first vowel is worn away as is most of the last. The name is not known from the later record, though the first element appears elsewhere in the Ogam corpus in the name COVAGNI. Ref. M. 96, P. 2

11.   Also from Ballyknock, this inscription presents enormous difficulties owing to the faint nature of its execution and subsequent weathering. It runs up the left-hand arris as the stone stands today. Macalister's reading was DRUTIQULI MAQI MAQI-RODAGNI, but he did draw attention to its faint nature, arguing that it was made as inconspicuous as possible to 'evade hostile observation'. Very few of the letters of Macalister's reading are clear to the observer today. The best the present writer could make of it was D[ ]g[ ]Te/iQUL[ ]Q. . . with indeterminate vowels in the gaps between the consonants. If Macalister's reading is correct, the first name appears to bear the element later appearing as the noun *drúth* 'jester', though nothing corresponding to the full name here is attested. The sequence MAQI MAQI is well known in Ogam inscriptions (see stone no. 18 below); the second MAQI in such cases does not express a filial relationship but rather forms part of a name with the following element, whence the hyphen in MAQI-RODAGNI (see the MAQI-ERCIAS of the next stone). RODAGNI is known from the later record in the form *Rúadán*, diminutive of *rúad* 'red'. Ref. M. 87, P. 1.

12.   This stone is the only one in the Cork collection which is not from Co. Cork. It was found on the top of a low cairn by the Rev P. Canon Power in Seemochuda, near Lismore, Co. Waterford and brought to the College for protection. The inscription runs up the left-hand arris, around the top and down the opposite side and

though deeply cut it is much weathered and difficult to make out. The reading is possibly eRcaGNI MAc/q[I] e[R]CIAS, the last name being the same as the first element in ERCAGNI. If so, one should possibly read ERCAGNI MAQI-ERCIAS, i.e. treating the last two words as part of a single name, the filial relationship being expressed by a possessive genitive construction rather than by the word for 'son'. Both names are attested later in the forms *Ercán*, and *Mac-Erce*. Ref. M. 262, P. 13.

13. The Ballyknock series recontinues with this stone, the inscription on which is very finely executed and runs up the middle of the left-hand arris reading ANM MeDDOGENI. The formula ANM X is well known in the Ogam corpus and appears to be a late development; it is not attested in Wales. The first word, corresponding to later Old Irish nom. sg. *ainm* 'name', is an exception to the rule that words in Ogam inscriptions are in the genitive. It may mean 'inscription' in this context, just as the phrase *ainm n-oguim* in later Irish means 'an inscription in the Ogam character'. The name MEDDO-GENI bears two well-known elements, viz. the word for 'mead' (Old Irish *mid*, gen. *medo*) and the patronymical suffix *-gen-* 'born of', and appears in later Irish in the form *Midgen*. Ref. M. 95, P. 12.

14. This is the smallest of the Ballyknock series of stones and its inscription presents numerous difficulties. Macalister's earlier reading [A]NM DULICCI MACI EBR[A]S[I] was revised to LAMADILICCI MAC MAIC BROCC in his Corpus. The inscription runs up the left-hand arris and across the top, the last letter being duplicated at the back of the top right-hand side (not visible today owing to the position of the stone). This writer's reading was: L[A]MaDULICCi MAC[ ]CBROC. The last name may correspond to later Irish *brocc* 'badger', attested elsewhere in the Ogam corpus in the forms BROCI and BROCAGNI (later *Brocc* and *Broccán*), though one would have expected *BRUCC (corresponding to the later gen. *Bruicc*) if the inscription post-dates the loss of –I. The first name is not known from the later record. Ref. M. 83, P. 11.

15. This stone from the Ballyknock series bears a badly worn inscription reading up on the rear left-hand arris as it now stands. The reading recorded by Macalister and Power is DOMMO MACU/I VEDUCERI, with the possibility that the first word might

be DEGO. The vowels are very difficult to make out and the present writer could only be sure of D[ ]MM[ ]MACi [ ]eRI with a lone E low down on the right hand arris. DOMMO is unknown in the later record though DEGO would correspond to Old Irish *daig*, gen. *dego* 'fire', which does appear as a personal name. It is tempting to see the Old Irish name *Fidchuire* (lit. 'wood-putter') in VEDUCERI, but the expected spelling in that case would be *Viducori*. Ref. M. 94, P. 10.

16.   This, the eighth stone of the Ballyknock series, bears a refreshingly clear and distinct, though finely executed, inscription on its left-hand arris reading CRONUN MAC BAIT. The inscription bears no case-ending (witness the MAC for earlier MAQQI) and is clearly late morphologically. The final name corresponds to Old Irish *báeth* 'foolish', attested as a personal name. The name CRONAN is found elsewhere in Ogam (from an earlier *Cronagni*) and corresponds to later *Crónán*, diminutive to *crón* 'brown'. The spelling on this inscription (viz. the –UN) is peculiar. Ref. M. 90, P. 9.

17.   Also from Ballyknock, the inscription on this stone is more boldly executed than the last with long deep scores and what remains of it is in good condition. It reads up the left-hand arris to a break in the stone and continues on the top as follows: ACTO MAQi[ ]MAGO. The first name is attested later as *Acht* and as the first element in *Achtán* (related to Old Irish *aigid* 'drives'). If MAGO were complete it would preserve the early vocalism of the word for 'slave', Old Irish nom. *m(a)ug* < *magu-*, gen. *mogo* (for an expected *mago*) < *magōs*. Ref. M. 92, P. 8.

18.   The inscription on this stone, the second last of the Ballyknock series, is boldly executed and in fair condition today. It reads up the left-hand arris to the top and continues on the lower right-hand side reading again to the top as follows:
CLIUCOANAS MAQi MAQi-TR[E]Ni. The last name, if correctly read, is the well-known *Mac-Tréoin* of later Irish, the second element being Old Irish *trén* 'strong (man), warrior'. The first name is peculiar as it stands and one wonders whether the OA is not an error for U, viz. –CUNAS, the well-known gen. sg. of the word for 'hound', Old Irish *cú*, gen. sg. *con*. Its first element is not clear. On the sequence MAQI MAQI see stone no. 11 above. Ref. M. 86, P. 7.

19.   The Ballyknock series ends with this stone. Its inscription runs up the left-hand arris to the top of the stone, where the last three notches of the final vowel are duplicated. It is clear and deeply cut reading BRANAN MAQI oQOLI. The name BRANAN (earlier *BRANAGNI) is a diminutive of the BRANI on stone no. 6 and is attested later as *Branán*. The last name may have a long or short O- and correspond to the name later attested as *Úachall* or to the *Ochall* in *Mac-Ochaill*, equated by Marstrander with Gallo-Latin *opulus* 'field maple'. If the latter, one might be tempted to read MAQI-OQOLI 'devotee of the field maple' (compare *Mac-Dara* 'devotee of the oak tree' and see the comments on stone no. 12 above). Ref. M. 88, P. 6.

20.   This stone was found in 1841 in Tuligmore in the barony of East Muskerry, Co, Cork. The disposition of the inscription is a little unusual, probably owing to the irregular shape of the stone. The reading given here begins on the middle angle (in the spall) reading up and continues on the right, again reading up:
MAQI LAS?OG, B/M[ ]TTM[ ]Cge. A downward reading on the right angle would produce egS[ ]MVV[ ]?/M, which is equally obscure. Macalister's original reading was EGSAMVVA MAQI LASKOGI but in the *Corpus* he read MAQILASPOG B TTMACDE and rather fancifully interpreted the B TT as an abbreviation of Latin *benedicat*, translating the inscription 'May the Son of God (MAC DE) bless Bishop Maqil' (MAQIL ASPOG). It is safe to say that few would go along with this interpretation today. The character following the S on the middle angle looks like the first of the supplementary characters (see stone no. 5 above) in the form ⋌ rather than X, but it is at best uncertain. Ref. M. 127, P. 23.

21.   This lintel from a souterrain in Glenawillin, five miles north of Midleton, Co. Cork, is unusual (though not unique) in bearing two independent inscriptions reading up the left-hand and right-hand sides respectively. As it stands today the stone is back-to-front viz. à viz. the sketch in Macalister's *Corpus*, i.e. Macalister's sinister inscription reads up the rear left arris on the stone as one faces it. This inscription is more boldly executed than the other and reads: BRuSC[ ]DOVALeSC. . . The left side of the scores of the R are not visible but the restoration BRUSCO MAQI DOVALESCI seems

reasonable. The inscription on the right arris is finely executed and reads COLOMAGNi [ ]V[ ]DU[ ]U. . . Macalister read COLO-MAGNI AVI DUCAGNI in his early publication, later COLOMAGNI AVI DUCURI. The name BRUSCO is well-known in Ogam and may correspond to later *brosc* 'thunder'; DOVALESCI is also later known, as *Duiblesc*, while COLOMAGNI corresponds to Old Irish *Colmán*, diminutive to *colum* 'dove', < Latin *columba*. AVI, Old Irish (nom.) *aue* 'grandson, descendant' is a common formula word in the Ogams. Ref. M. 63, P. 17.

22.   This formed part of a stone circle in Glounagloch, barony of East Muskerry, Co. Cork, and after serving for a while as a lintel in a pig-stye, came to the College through the Royal Cork Institution. As it stands today the stone is upside-down, the inscription reading down the lower part of the right-hand arris instead of up the upper left-hand side. The reading is clear but the inscription is incomplete; note the interference with all letters after the first six: CUNAGUSSOS MA. . . The name CUNAGUSSOS is later attested as (nom.) *Congus* and is compounded of the two elements *cuno-* 'hound' (Old Irish *cú*) and *gussu-* 'strength' (Old Irish *gus*), meaning 'having the strength of a hound'. Ref. M. 107, P. 19.

23.   Found built into the structure of St Olan's Church, near Aghabullogue, barony of East Muskerry, Co. Cork, this stone also came to the College from the Royal Cork Institution. Unfortunately the stone was badly damaged in its second life and the inscription is for the most part unintelligible. Reading up the right-hand arris, the top third, beginning just above the spall on the left, appears to yield VIDETT[ ]S with space for an A or an O before the S. Below this section several scores are visible on the B face but it seems pointless to speculate as to what the original reading was. Macalister's ANM NETACUNAS CELI VIDETTAS is very risky, except for the last name, which, however, is not known from the later record. Ref. M. 105, P. 20.

24.   This stone was found by the Rev. Canon Power built into the gate-pier of a farm wall in Bishop's Island, Co. Cork. The reading is up the right-hand angle as the stone stands today and the inscription is incomplete: OLAGNI MAq. . . The first three scores of the expected Q of MAQQI are visible at the top of the stone. The name

may correspond to Gaulish *Ollognus* and contain the element later attested in Irish as *oll* 'great'. If the O is long it may correspond to Old Irish *úall* 'pride', from which names like *Úallach* and *Úallachán* were formed. There is a possibility, however, that O was not the original initial as the surface of the stone is flaked away before it. Ref. M. 61, P. 22.

25. This stone was found in a bog in Carrigagulla, barony of West Muskerry, Co. Cork. The inscription is badly worn and spalled and reads up both angles. Right angle, up and top: DOVEd/ti [MA]q[I] LoCARENAs. . . Only three scores of the expected final S are visible. Left angle, up and top: C[ ]u mAQi CULiDOVI. For the first word here Macalister reads CELI. The name DOVETI is attested elsewhere in Ogam. Its first element is the same as that in the DOVALESCI of stone no. 21 (Old Irish *dub* 'black') and it may correspond to later Irish *Dubad* or Dubthae, depending on whether it is an *o*- or an *io*-stem. CULI-DOVI presumably corresponds to Old Irish *Cúldub* with the same DOV = *dub* 'black' element and a first element corresponding to Old Irish *cúl* 'back (of head)'. The other name is not known from the later record. Ref. M. 128 (not in P.).

26a/b. Stones 26a and 26b, the latter clamped to the wall above and to the right of the former, were originally one, and formed the second lintel in the souterrain in Knockshanawee. As it stands stone 26a is upside-down and the inscription, which is difficult to make out, reads down the lower right-hand side to the bottom as follows: GRi[ ]GGN. . . The continuation on no. 26b reads up the outer angle and yields . . .CERC. . ., with one vowel notch visible before the first C. Macalister restores the full inscription as: GRIMIGGN[I MAQI] CERC . . . The first name is diminutive in structure with its GN suffix, but it has not been identified in later sources. The ending of the second name is lost but the equation with Old Irish *cerc* 'hen' suggests itself. Ref. M. 114, P. 16/18.

27. This is the last stone of the Knockshanawee series and it completes the College collection. It formed the innermost lintel in the souterrain and its inscription is very faint and quite difficult to read. Note the unusual spacing between the words. As it stands the reading is down the right-hand angle as follows: uCANAVVI

MA[ ] L[ ]N. Macalister read MICANAVVI MAQ LUGUN[I]. If he is right, the person recorded here may be a brother of the man recorded on stone no. 5. For the name LUGUNI see stone no. 5. The first name is unclear. Ref. M. 112, P. 21.

Select Bibliography

For a detailed bibliography of works on Ogam up to 1991 *see*: McManus *A guide to Ogam*, Maynooth Monographs 4, 1991, p. 186 ff.

Important works published since then include:

Cox, R. (1999): *The language of the Ogam inscriptions of Scotland*, Aberdeen.

de hÓir, S. (1998): 'Late Scholastic Ogham from Kilkenny', *Dublin and beyond the Pale; Studies in honour of Patrick Healy*, ed. Conleth Manning, Bray, 257–64.

Forsyth, K. S. (1997): *Languages in Pictland*, Utrecht.

Moore, Fionnbarr: 'Munster Ogham stones: siting, context and funstion' in M.S. Monk and J. Sheehan (eds.), *Early Medieval Munster: archaeology, history and society*, Cork University Press (1998)

Sims-Williams, P. (1992): 'The additional letters of the Ogam alphabet', *Cambridge Medieval Celtic Studies*, 23, 29–95.

(1993): 'Some problems in deciphering the Early Irish Ogam alphabet', *Transactions of the Philological Society*, 91, 133–80.

Swift, C. (1997): *Ogam stones and the earliest Irish Christians*, Maynooth Monographs, Series Minor 2.

Thomas, C. (1994): *And shall these mute stones speak? Post-Roman inscriptions in western Britain*, Cardiff.

Ziegler, S. (1994): Die Sprache der altirischen Ogam-inschriften, Göttingen.

The reader might also like to consult Fios Feasa's CD Rom *Ogham*, which offers readings of all Ogam inscriptions together with commentary, map-references, photographs, a good introduction to the subject and connections to important websites.